T0051501

76ers LEGENDS ALPHABET

Words by Robin Feiner

A is for **A**llen Iverson. The Answer's hip-hop style and legendary crossover made him one of the game's most influential players ever. Dominating with determination and strength instead of size, A.I. was a four-time league scoring leader and three-time steals leader. As the 2000–01 MVP, he led Philly to the 2001 Finals.

B is for **B**illy Cunningham. A legendary leaper, The Kangaroo Kid's intense sixth-man play helped Philadelphia win the 1967 title. Rising to star starter, he earned four All-Star nods with Philly from 1968–72. Coach Cunningham then led the Sixers to three Finals in four seasons from 1979–83, winning in his third try.

C is for Charles Barkley. The Round Mound of Rebound was smaller than other bigs. But The Chuckster's all-around game made him an all-time great, with six All-Star appearances in eight Sixers seasons from 1984–92. Though the power forward's habit of speaking his mind sometimes landed him in trouble.

D is for **D**arryl Dawkins. The first player drafted out of high school straight to the NBA, Chocolate Thunder quickly went from manchild to fan favorite, breaking backboards with ferocious nicknamed dunks. The giant center helped Philly make three finals in his seven Sixers seasons.

E is for Joel **E**mbiid. This Cameroonian center's legendary play is the reward for trusting the Process. A skilled big man who can score from inside, midrange, or downtown, Embiid's dominant offensive and defensive performances helped him win the 2022-23 MVP award.

F is for World B. **F**ree. Free's flashy style and legendary rainbow jumper made him one of the game's original gunners and a legend across his four seasons in Philly. Lloyd Free was drafted by Philly in 1975, with the Prince of Mid-Air providing All-World bench scoring and showmanship.

G is for Hal Greer.
Greer's legendary jumper –
even on free throws – helped
him lead the team in playoff
scoring during the Sixers'
1967 NBA championship run.
Playing his entire 15-year
career with the franchise, the
consistent Hall-of-Fame guard
earned 10 straight All-Star
nods from 1960–70. He retired
as a top-10 NBA scorer.

H is for **H**ersey Hawkins. Hawk only missed seven games in his five Philly seasons from 1988–93. His scoring helped him earn an All-Star appearance in his third season, but he was also disruptive on defense. His legendary nine-steal effort against the Boston Celtics in a 1991 game proved it.

I is for Irv Kosloff.
Fans were distraught after
the Philadelphia Warriors
left for California in 1962.
But Kosloff, a native of Philly,
made sure the city didn't
go without hoops for long.
He bought the Syracuse
Nationals and moved them
home to become the 76ers
the next year.

J is for Julius Erving.
Dr. J was an All-Star in each of his 11 Sixers seasons from 1976–87 and guided the team to four Finals appearances, finally triumphing in 1983. His sky-high gliding, including his legendary Rock the Baby dunk and baseline wizardry, brought the sport to dizzying new heights.

K is for Red **K**err.
Kerr played 11 seasons
for the franchise from
1954–65. He was one
of the most legendary
players the game has seen,
with his record of 844
straight games played
standing until 1983. The
center formed a formidable
pair with fellow big
man Dolph Schayes.

L is for Little Mo.
While *Moses Malone* and
***Julius Erving* grabbed much**
of the spotlight, point guard
***Maurice Cheeks* orchestrated**
the offense and locked up
opposing guards to help lead
the Sixers to the 1983 title.
He left Philly after 11 seasons
as the franchise's all-time
assists and steals leader.

M is for **M**oses Malone.
His legendary "Fo' Fo' Fo'"
playoff prediction – which
missed by one game – was
about the only thing Big Mo
did wrong during the 1982–83
season in which he won both
the league and Finals MVP.
Behind signature quickness
and strength, Malone led
the league in rebounds from
1982–85 with Philly.

N is for **N**erlens Noel.
A Process legend, Noel
was one of the many moving
pieces of general manager
Sam Hinkie's rebuilding
puzzle. Some view the
talented shot-blocker's 2013
selection at No. 6 as the
beginning of Hinkie's years-
long attempt to add big-
time talent through high
draft picks.

O is for Kevin **O**llie. This guard wasn't considered a star. But he had a reputation for having a legendarily high basketball IQ and was a great teammate. In 280 games across three different stints in Philly between 1999–2008, Ollie provided a calming presence off the bench.

P is for Paul Seymour.
He played 11 years with
the Syracuse Nationals' from
1949–60, including a stint as
player-coach from 1956–60.
Even before taking over, this
legend led by example. A
three-time All-Star, Seymour
logged a team-high 41
minutes per game during
the Nationals 1955
championship season

Q is for Equality.
From broadcaster Kate Scott becoming the team's first female play-by-play announcer in 2021 to hosting community events in addition to an annual Pride Night game, the Sixers organization stands for equality. And that's nothing short of legendary.

R is for Theo **R**atliff.
This legend battled some
of the baddest bigs in the
league. His All-Star 2000–01
season was his best in Philly.
He led the league with 3.7
blocks per game, before a
wrist injury caused the Sixers
to trade him before their
2001 Finals run.

S is for Dolph Schayes.
This center's legendary hook shot made him one of the sport's first stars. Spending his entire 1949–64 career with the franchise, Schayes was a 12-time All-Star and retired holding the team points and rebounds records. He was a player-coach his final season – the team's first in Philly.

T is for **Andrew Toney.** This fearless shooting guard rose to the occasion whenever the Sixers played the powerhouse Boston Celtics in the 1980s. This earned him the legendary nickname The Boston Strangler. A matchup nightmare, Toney was a two-time All-Star before injuries cut his career short at the young age of 30.

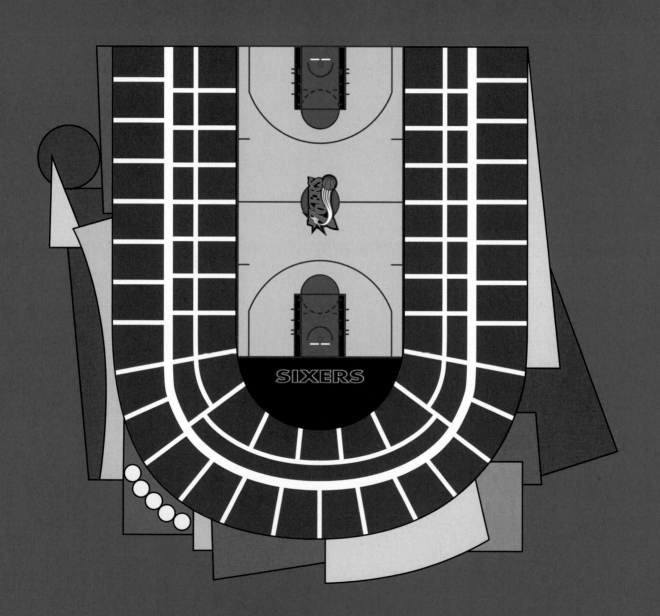

U is for First **U**nion Center. The name of the Sixers' home from 1998–2003, this arena hosted some of the team's most iconic moments. Many of these came in the magical 2000–01 season in which the team reached the Finals, including Allen Iverson's legendary 54-point performance against the Raptors in the second round of the playoffs.

V is for Tom Van Arsdale. His 929 games played without a single playoff appearance is a record nobody wants. Van Arsdale averaged 18.6 points per game with Philly, but was on some legendarily bad Sixers teams. Joining the team in 1973 before a '74 trade to Atlanta, the Sixers went 34–83 during his stint.

W is for **W**ilt Chamberlain. Chamberlain's legendary Sixers career saw him win league MVP every year during his three full seasons with the team from 1964–67. Nearly unstoppable, The Big Dipper is arguably the greatest offensive player in history. In the 1966–67 season, he led Philly to a then-record 68 wins and the championship.

X is for Alex Hannum.
He coached the Sixers to
three Eastern Finals and
one Finals appearance in
his five seasons in charge.
He asked superstar Wilt
Chamberlain to emphasize
passing and defense for the
team's legendary 1966–67
seasons, during which the
Sixers won a then-record
68 games and the title.

Y is for George **Yardley.**
Yardley played the final
88 games of his legendary
Hall-of-Fame career with
the Syracuse Nationals from
1958–60. The man known
as The Bird was one of his
era's greatest scorers, and
was an All-Star both seasons
with the team.

Z is for Marc Zumoff.
A local legend in Philly,
Zoo was the TV play-by-play
voice of the Sixers from
1994–2021. A native of the
city, Zumoff's Philly fandom
shined through in his calls as
he guided viewers through
some of the team's highest
highs and lowest lows.

The ever-expanding legendary library

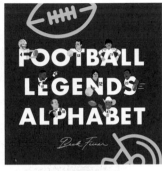

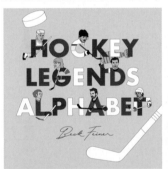

EXPLORE THESE LEGENDARY ALPHABETS & MORE AT WWW.ALPHABETLEGENDS.COM

76ERS LEGENDS ALPHABET
www.alphabetlegends.com

Published by Alphabet Legends Pty Ltd in 2023
Created by Beck Feiner
Copyright © Alphabet Legends Pty Ltd 2023

Printed and bound in China.

9780645487091

The right of Beck Feiner to be identified as the author
and illustrator of this work has been asserted by her in
accordance with the Copyright Amendment (Moral Rights)
Act 2000.

This work is copyright. Apart from any use as permitted
under the Copyright Act 1968, no part may be reproduced,
copied, scanned, stored in a retrieval system, recorded or
transmitted, in any form or by any means, without the prior
use of the publisher.

This book is not officially endorsed by the people and
characters depicted.